Electoral Earthquake

The ANC's Rise and Collapse after 2024

MICHAEL MOKOBANE

Published by Michael Mokobane

DEDICATION

To the resilient people of South Africa, whose voices echo through history and whose unwavering spirit fuels the hope for a better tomorrow. To every voter who believed in change, to those who refused to stay silent, and to the dreamers who envision a nation built on integrity, justice, and true democracy. And to my family and friends who have supported me through this journey — your belief in me has been my greatest strength. This book is for you and for all who strive to understand and shape the future of our beautiful country.

CONTENTS

ACKNOWLEDGMENTS

A special thank you to my family and friends for their unwavering support and encouragement. Your belief in me has been a constant source of strength. Your encouragement has been my guiding light throughout this journey. To the people of South Africa — this book is for you. Your resilience, courage, and determination are what keep the spirit of our democracy alive. Your stories, struggles, and victories inspired every page, reminding me that our nation's journey is as profound as it is complex.
Ngiyabonga, ke a leboga, thank you. Let's continue to learn, reflect, and build the future together.

INTRODUCTION

South Africa's political landscape

The story of South Africa's political landscape is one deeply rooted in the complex interplay of historical struggle, human resilience, and the hope for a better future. Emerging from the oppressive shadow of apartheid in 1994, the country was heralded as a global beacon of reconciliation and democracy. South Africa's transition was not merely a shift in governance; it was a seismic social transformation, one that dismantled institutionalised racial segregation and set the stage for a new era of equality, dignity, and opportunity. The first democratic election, held on 27 April 1994, marked the culmination of decades of struggle, sacrifice, and the dreams of a nation yearning for liberation. It was a day that etched itself into the collective memory of South Africans, both those who voted for the first time and those who had endured the brutality of apartheid.

At the forefront of this monumental change stood the African National Congress (ANC), a liberation movement that had been the heartbeat of the resistance against apartheid for decades. Founded in 1912, the ANC had long championed the cause of equality and freedom. Its leaders, such as Nelson Mandela, Oliver Tambo, and Walter Sisulu, became symbols of the fight against injustice, embodying the unyielding spirit of a people determined to overcome oppression. By the time the apartheid regime began to collapse under the weight of international sanctions, internal unrest, and the moral bankruptcy of its policies, the ANC was poised to lead South Africa into a new democratic dawn.

The post-apartheid political landscape was both promising and fraught with challenges. The ANC's victory in 1994 was overwhelming, winning 62.65% of the vote, a clear indication of the faith South Africans placed in the movement that had delivered them from the clutches of apartheid. Nelson Mandela, affectionately known as "Madiba," became the country's first black president, a symbol of unity who sought to heal the wounds of the past through reconciliation and nation-building. The Truth and Reconciliation Commission (TRC), chaired by Archbishop Desmond Tutu, exemplified the spirit of the time—an attempt to confront the horrors of the past while laying the groundwork for a collective future.

However, the promises of the Rainbow Nation were not without their complications. The legacy of apartheid—manifested in vast socio-economic inequalities, racial tensions, and systemic poverty— cast a long shadow over the fledgling democracy. While the ANC championed ambitious policies such as the Reconstruction and Development Programme (RDP), designed to redress past injustices through housing, education, and basic services, the sheer magnitude of the task often outstripped the resources and capacity available. For many South Africans, particularly those in rural areas and townships, the dream of liberation remained elusive as poverty and unemployment persisted.

The Birth of the ANC as a Governing Force

When the ANC transitioned from a liberation movement to a governing party, it carried with it the weight of immense expectation. For decades, it had been the voice of the oppressed, articulating the aspirations of millions and inspiring hope in the face of despair. But governance, unlike resistance, demanded not just ideals but also practical solutions to complex problems. The ANC was now tasked with transforming its revolutionary ethos into a sustainable framework for leading a diverse and divided nation.

The early years of ANC governance were characterised by a delicate balancing act. On one hand, the party sought to deliver on the promises of liberation by addressing the socio-economic disparities that apartheid had entrenched. On the other, it had to ensure that the fragile democracy remained stable, which required navigating relationships with a range of stakeholders, including international investors, minority groups, and political opposition. The

Government of National Unity, which included members of the National Party and Inkatha Freedom Party, reflected the compromises necessary to foster inclusivity and prevent the country from descending into post-conflict instability.

Under Mandela's leadership, the ANC focused on creating a legislative framework that dismantled the legal remnants of apartheid while laying the foundation for a more equitable society. Landmark policies such as the Land Restitution Act and the Employment Equity Act aimed to address historical injustices, while efforts to reform education and healthcare sought to uplift the nation's most vulnerable. Yet, even as Mandela's presidency was lauded globally, cracks in the ANC's governance began to emerge. The realities of bureaucracy, inefficiency, and corruption started to rear their heads, foreshadowing challenges that would grow more pronounced in subsequent administrations.

By the time Thabo Mbeki assumed the presidency in 1999, the ANC had firmly entrenched itself as the dominant political force in South Africa. The party enjoyed broad support across racial and class lines, its liberation credentials lending it moral authority. Mbeki's tenure was marked by a technocratic approach, focusing on macroeconomic stability and positioning South Africa as a key player on the African continent and the global stage. However, this period also highlighted the ANC's struggles to reconcile its dual identity as a party of the people and a governing institution operating within a capitalist framework.

While the ANC's first decade in power saw significant strides in infrastructure development, basic service delivery, and the creation of a constitutional democracy, the party's transformation into a governing force was not without growing pains. Factionalism, the centralisation of power, and the increasing disconnect between the leadership and grassroots members hinted at deeper structural issues within the organisation. Nevertheless, the ANC's grip on South African politics remained unshaken, its liberation history continuing to serve as a powerful narrative that resonated with the electorate.

As the 2000s progressed, the ANC's dominance began to face subtle but significant challenges. The economic policies of the Mbeki era, while stabilising the economy, were criticised for failing to address unemployment and inequality meaningfully. Meanwhile, internal divisions within the party, exacerbated by the rise of Jacob Zuma and his populist rhetoric, signalled a shift in the ANC's internal dynamics. What had once been a unified liberation movement began to fracture under the pressures of governance, personal ambition, and ideological divergence.

By 2024, the ANC found itself at a crossroads. The party that had brought freedom to South Africa was now grappling with the realities of its own shortcomings. Its rise to power had been meteoric, but its trajectory as a governing force was riddled with contradictions, compromises, and failures to adapt to the evolving needs of the nation. As the electorate's patience wore thin, the stage was set for the seismic political shift that would redefine South Africa's political landscape and forever alter the course of its history.

Part 1: Historical Context

1 The Rise of the ANC

The African National Congress (ANC) stands as a symbol of South Africa's liberation struggle, embodying decades of resistance against systemic oppression and racial segregation. Its journey from a revolutionary movement to the governing force of a democratic nation is a story steeped in sacrifice, resilience, and profound historical significance. For many South Africans, the ANC is more than a political party; it is a custodian of liberation and the promise of a brighter, equitable future. Yet, the story of its rise is as complex as the history of the country it sought to free.

Liberation Struggle and Mandela's Presidency

The roots of the ANC's struggle date back to its founding in 1912, when it was established as the South African Native National Congress. The movement aimed to unify black South Africans in their fight against the injustices of colonial rule and, later, apartheid. From its early years, the ANC adopted a strategy of non-violent resistance, championing the rights of the disenfranchised through petitions, public demonstrations, and dialogue with the ruling authorities. However, as apartheid's oppressive policies intensified following the National Party's rise to power in 1948, the ANC realised that its efforts required a more radical approach.

The 1950s and 1960s were pivotal decades in the ANC's transformation. Under the leadership of figures like Oliver Tambo, Walter Sisulu, and Nelson Mandela, the ANC embraced mass mobilisation and civil disobedience campaigns, epitomised by the Defiance Campaign and the adoption of the Freedom Charter in 1955. The Freedom Charter was a ground-breaking document that articulated the vision of a democratic and non-racial South Africa, encapsulating the aspirations of millions who longed for dignity, equality, and justice. However, the apartheid regime's response was brutal, marked by increasing repression, arrests, and the infamous Sharpeville Massacre of 1960. The massacre not only shocked the nation but also forced the ANC to rethink its strategy. Shortly thereafter, the party was banned, driving its leaders underground or into exile.

It was during this period of suppression that the ANC formed Umkhonto we Sizwe (MK), its armed wing, as a response to the regime's violent crackdown on peaceful protests. Leaders like Mandela, who was arrested in 1962 and later sentenced to life imprisonment during the Rivonia Trial, became symbols of resistance. Despite the ANC's leadership operating in exile or imprisonment, the organisation continued to inspire resistance within South Africa. Internationally, it garnered widespread support as the apartheid state became increasingly isolated due to economic sanctions, cultural boycotts, and diplomatic pressure.

The collapse of apartheid in the early 1990s was the

culmination of relentless internal and external pressure. The unbanning of the ANC in 1990, coupled with the release of Nelson Mandela after 27 years of incarceration, marked the beginning of a new chapter. Negotiations between the ANC and the National Party paved the way for South Africa's first democratic elections in 1994. The ANC, buoyed by its liberation legacy, secured an overwhelming victory, ushering in the presidency of Nelson Mandela. Mandela's tenure was not only a triumph of justice over oppression but also a masterclass in leadership and reconciliation.

Mandela's presidency from 1994 to 1999 was characterised by his unwavering commitment to nation-building and healing the wounds of apartheid. Initiatives like the Truth and Reconciliation Commission (TRC) sought to confront the past while fostering forgiveness and unity. Yet, Mandela's leadership went beyond symbolic gestures. Under his administration, the ANC laid the groundwork for rebuilding South Africa's fractured society, focusing on basic service delivery, education, housing, and healthcare. Programs like the Reconstruction and Development Programme (RDP) aimed to redress the socio-economic disparities entrenched by apartheid. Though Mandela stepped down after a single term, his legacy as a moral compass and unifier cemented the ANC's place in the hearts of many South Africans.

Consolidation of Power: The Mbeki Era

If Mandela's presidency was about healing and transition, Thabo Mbeki's tenure (1999–2008) represented an era of consolidation and modernisation. Mbeki inherited a nation still grappling with the legacies of apartheid—inequality, unemployment, and poverty—but his approach to governance differed significantly from his predecessor's. While Mandela emphasised reconciliation, Mbeki sought to position South Africa as a global economic player and leader on the African continent. This shift marked a new phase in the ANC's evolution as a governing force.

Mbeki was a technocrat, deeply intellectual and pragmatic. Under his leadership, South Africa adopted the Growth, Employment, and Redistribution (GEAR) strategy, a macroeconomic framework aimed at stabilising the economy, reducing debt, and attracting foreign investment. Mbeki's economic policies prioritised fiscal discipline and neoliberal reforms, which earned him praise from international investors but alienated segments of the ANC's traditional support base, particularly trade unions and grassroots activists. While GEAR succeeded in fostering economic growth, critics argued that it did little to address structural inequalities or create jobs for the millions left behind by the apartheid economy.

On the international stage, Mbeki championed African Renaissance—a vision for the continent's renewal through unity, self-reliance, and development. He played a pivotal role in the establishment of the African Union (AU) and the New Partnership for Africa's Development (NEPAD), asserting South Africa's leadership in peacekeeping and regional stability. Domestically, however, Mbeki's presidency was marred by controversies that exposed the ANC's internal contradictions and growing pains as a governing party.

One of the most contentious issues of Mbeki's presidency was his handling of the HIV/AIDS epidemic. His scepticism of mainstream scientific consensus and promotion of alternative treatments led to widespread criticism and, tragically, thousands of preventable deaths. This policy failure not only tarnished his administration but also highlighted the disconnect between the ANC's leadership and the realities faced by ordinary South Africans.

Despite these challenges, Mbeki's tenure saw significant progress in infrastructure development, housing, and education. South Africa's democratic institutions—its judiciary, parliament, and media—remained robust under his watch. However, the cracks within the ANC were beginning to show. Factionalism, driven by ideological differences, personal ambitions, and competing power blocs, became increasingly pronounced. The battle for succession between Mbeki and Jacob Zuma, his populist deputy, culminated in a dramatic split that would shape the ANC's trajectory in the years to come.

By the time Mbeki was recalled by the ANC in 2008, the seeds of the party's internal struggles had already been sown. While the ANC had successfully consolidated its power and entrenched itself as South Africa's dominant political force, its internal cohesion was deteriorating. The unity that had characterised its liberation struggle began to fragment under the pressures of governance, shifting alliances, and the compromises of power.

The Mbeki era represented both the high point of the ANC's dominance and the beginning of its internal unravelling. His administration's achievements and shortcomings reflected the broader challenges of transitioning from a liberation movement to a governing party in a complex and unequal society. As the ANC moved forward into the tumultuous years that followed, its rise to prominence stood as a testament to its history, but its cracks foreshadowed the electoral earthquake that would one day redefine its legacy.

2 The ANC's Golden Years

The period following the ANC's historic ascent to power in 1994 is often regarded as its golden years—a time when the party's liberation credentials translated into tangible hope and a renewed sense of possibility for millions of South Africans. Having won the first democratic elections with an overwhelming majority, the ANC carried the immense burden of expectations from a population that had endured centuries of systemic oppression and exclusion. It was a time of bold vision and ambitious goals, with the ANC pledging to transform South Africa into a nation of dignity, equality, and opportunity. These golden years, while marked by significant strides in service delivery and governance, were also riddled with challenges that foreshadowed the struggles the party would later face.

Service Delivery Successes

In its early years of governance, the ANC made commendable progress in addressing the most immediate needs of South Africa's previously marginalised communities. Central to its agenda was the Reconstruction and Development Programme (RDP), a comprehensive policy framework aimed at redressing the socio-economic imbalances left by apartheid. The RDP's primary focus was on improving access to housing, healthcare, education, water, and electricity for millions of South Africans who had been systematically excluded from these basic services.

One of the ANC's most visible successes during this period was its rapid rollout of housing projects. By the end of its first decade in power, the ANC government had built millions of subsidised houses, providing shelter to families who had lived in overcrowded informal settlements or under apartheid-era pass laws that restricted black ownership of property. These houses, often referred to as "RDP homes," became a symbol of the ANC's commitment to improving the lives of the poor. For many, owning a home for the first time represented more than just a roof over their heads—it was a profound assertion of dignity and belonging in a country that had systematically denied them both.

Access to electricity and clean water also saw remarkable improvements under ANC governance. Before 1994, black communities in rural areas and townships had been deliberately excluded from such services. The electrification programme, initiated in the mid-1990s, extended power to millions of households, transforming the daily lives of people who had relied on paraffin lamps and firewood. Similarly, water infrastructure projects ensured that millions of South Africans gained access to clean, piped water for the first time. These basic services, often taken for granted in wealthier suburbs, became lifelines for families in underprivileged areas, allowing them to live with greater safety and dignity.

Healthcare also saw significant strides under the ANC during its early years. The introduction of free healthcare for pregnant women and children under six marked a bold step in reducing maternal and child mortality rates. Clinics were built in remote rural areas, bringing medical services to communities that had long been neglected. Immunisation campaigns and HIV/AIDS awareness programmes, though initially limited in scope, began to lay the foundation for a more equitable public healthcare system. These interventions were instrumental in demonstrating the ANC's commitment to bridging the gap between South Africa's rich and poor.

Stumbling Blocks: Housing, Education, and Inequality

Despite these successes, the challenges of governing a deeply unequal society soon began to weigh heavily on the ANC. The task of undoing centuries of dispossession and marginalisation proved far more complex and resource-intensive than even the most optimistic planners could have anticipated. While the ANC's early efforts were laudable, they were often insufficient to meet the growing demands of an increasingly frustrated population.

Housing, once celebrated as a major success story, became a source of contention as the quality and sustainability of RDP homes came under scrutiny. Many houses were built quickly to meet numerical targets, but this haste often resulted in substandard construction. Cracks in walls, leaking roofs, and inadequate infrastructure became common complaints. For beneficiaries, the dream of owning a home sometimes turned into a nightmare of costly repairs and legal disputes with developers. Additionally, the pace of housing delivery slowed over time, leaving millions still waiting for their promised homes. Informal settlements continued to grow on the outskirts of cities, highlighting the government's inability to keep up with urbanisation and the demand for affordable housing.

Education was another area where the ANC faced significant challenges. While the party made impressive strides in increasing access to schooling, the quality of education in many public schools remained abysmal. Underfunded, overcrowded, and poorly resourced schools in rural areas and townships perpetuated cycles of poverty rather than breaking them. The apartheid-era education system, designed to limit opportunities for black South Africans, left a legacy that could not be dismantled overnight. The ANC struggled to address issues such as a lack of qualified teachers, outdated curricula, and inadequate infrastructure. Despite high enrolment rates, the poor performance of learners in critical areas like maths and science undermined their chances of success in higher education and the job market.

Inequality, perhaps the most stubborn of South Africa's socio-economic challenges, persisted despite the ANC's best efforts. The divide between rich and poor, urban and rural, black and white, remained glaringly evident. While the economy grew under Thabo Mbeki's administration, this growth often benefited a small elite, leaving millions of South Africans trapped in poverty. The rise of a black middle class, while celebrated as a sign of progress, could not overshadow the stark reality of widespread unemployment and underdevelopment in many communities. Youth unemployment, in particular, became a ticking time bomb, with a generation of young people increasingly disillusioned by the lack of opportunities.

As the ANC's golden years drew to a close, the party's achievements were undeniable, but so too were its shortcomings. It had laid the foundation for a more equitable South Africa, but the cracks in its policies and implementation strategies were beginning to show. Service delivery protests became a common feature of the political landscape, reflecting the growing frustration of citizens who felt that the promises of liberation had not yet been fully realised. While the ANC remained dominant at the ballot box, the seeds of discontent had been sown, setting the stage for the challenges and internal contradictions that would later define its trajectory.

In many ways, the ANC's golden years were a microcosm of South Africa itself: a period of remarkable progress tempered by deep-seated challenges. It was a time of hope and ambition, but also of missed opportunities and rising tensions. As the party moved forward, it carried the weight of both its successes and its failures, navigating an increasingly complex and demanding political landscape. For millions of South Africans, the question lingered: could the ANC deliver on its promises, or would it falter under the weight of its own history?

3 Early Warning Signs

The ANC's transition from a liberation movement to a governing party was never going to be without challenges, but the early warning signs of its eventual decline began to emerge during the presidency of Jacob Zuma. It was a period marked by deepening corruption, internal factionalism, and leadership struggles that chipped away at the party's moral authority and connection to its base. For many South Africans, the ANC's promise of liberation started to feel hollow, its reputation tarnished by scandals and a growing perception that it had lost touch with the people it claimed to serve. These issues, compounded over time, would lay the foundation for the seismic political shift that unfolded in the 2024 elections.

Zuma's Presidency and the Guptagate Scandal

Jacob Zuma's rise to power in 2009 was both a testament to the ANC's internal divisions and a harbinger of the challenges to come. Zuma, a charismatic and populist figure, presented himself as a man of the people, a stark contrast to the technocratic and often aloof Thabo Mbeki. His ability to mobilise grassroots support, particularly within the ANC's powerful alliance with the Congress of South African

Trade Unions (COSATU) and the South African Communist Party (SACP), helped him secure the presidency. However, Zuma's tenure would become synonymous with corruption and mismanagement, culminating in one of the most infamous scandals in South Africa's democratic history: Guptagate.

The Guptagate scandal epitomised the intersection of political power and personal enrichment that came to define Zuma's presidency. The Gupta family, a wealthy business dynasty with close ties to Zuma, was accused of wielding undue influence over government decisions, a phenomenon widely referred to as "state capture." Evidence surfaced of lucrative government contracts being awarded to Gupta-linked companies, often bypassing due process and at the expense of the public purse. The scale of the corruption was staggering, with estimates suggesting that billions of rands were siphoned off from state-owned enterprises such as Eskom, Transnet, and South African Airways.

The term "state capture" gained traction as the Gupta family's influence became increasingly visible, from their ability to dictate ministerial appointments to their extravagant use of public resources, such as landing a private jet at a national key point like the Waterkloof Air Force Base. For ordinary South Africans, the revelations were both shocking and deeply disheartening. The ANC, once a symbol of integrity and resistance against apartheid, now seemed complicit in the erosion of the very democracy it had fought to establish.

Zuma's presidency also coincided with a broader culture of impunity within the ANC. Allegations of corruption were not limited to the national level but permeated provincial and municipal governments. Service delivery protests became commonplace, as communities grew increasingly frustrated with the mismanagement and misappropriation of funds meant to improve their lives. Instead of addressing these concerns, Zuma's administration often dismissed criticism as part of a political agenda against him, further alienating the electorate.

ANC's Internal Power Battles

While corruption eroded the ANC's public image, internal factionalism and leadership struggles began to destabilise the party from within. The unity that had characterised the ANC during its liberation struggle gave way to deep divisions, fuelled by competing interests and ideologies. These battles were not merely disagreements over policy but bitter power struggles that often played out in the public eye, exposing the party's internal weaknesses.

Zuma's presidency was a catalyst for these divisions. His rise to power had been built on the support of a coalition of factions within the ANC, but maintaining that coalition proved increasingly difficult. As allegations of corruption mounted, many within the party began to question whether Zuma's leadership was worth the damage it was causing to the ANC's reputation. The battle lines were drawn between those who supported Zuma, often referred to as the "premier league" faction, and those who sought to distance the ANC from his tainted legacy.

One of the most contentious leadership struggles unfolded in the lead-up to the ANC's elective conference in 2017. Cyril Ramaphosa, a long-time ANC stalwart and former trade union leader, positioned himself as a reformist candidate, promising to root out corruption and restore the party's integrity. His campaign was met with fierce resistance from Zuma's allies, who feared that a Ramaphosa presidency would lead to a reckoning for those implicated in state capture. The conference ultimately saw Ramaphosa narrowly elected as ANC president, a victory that highlighted the deep divisions within the party.

The aftermath of Ramaphosa's victory was marked by ongoing factional battles, as the ANC struggled to present a unified front. Efforts to hold those implicated in corruption accountable were often stymied by resistance from within the party, reflecting the extent to which patronage networks had become entrenched. The tension between reformists and loyalists to Zuma created a paralysing environment, where the ANC appeared more focused on internal squabbles than on governing the country effectively.

For the electorate, these power battles further undermined confidence in the ANC. The party that had once stood for unity and collective struggle now seemed consumed by self-interest and infighting. Communities grappling with unemployment, poverty, and failing public services saw little evidence that the ANC was capable of addressing their concerns. The gap between the party's leadership and its grassroots support widened, with many long-time supporters beginning to question whether the ANC could still deliver on its promises.

The Warning Signs

The corruption, factionalism, and leadership struggles that characterised Zuma's presidency were not isolated events but part of a broader pattern that signalled the ANC's decline. While the party remained dominant at the polls, its support base was gradually eroding, particularly in urban areas where frustration with poor service delivery and corruption was most acute. The 2016 local government elections were a wake-up call, as the ANC lost control of major metros like Johannesburg, Tshwane, and Nelson Mandela Bay. These losses highlighted the growing disillusionment among voters, a trend that would accelerate in the years leading up to the 2024 electoral earthquake.

The ANC's inability to address these early warning signs reflected deeper structural issues within the party. Its transformation from a liberation movement to a governing party had not been accompanied by the necessary institutional reforms to ensure accountability and transparency. Instead, the party became a vehicle for personal enrichment and factional power plays, undermining its ability to govern effectively.

By the time the 2024 elections arrived, the damage had been done. The ANC's golden years were a distant memory, overshadowed by the scandals and struggles of the Zuma era. For many South Africans, the party that had delivered freedom was now synonymous with failure, corruption, and betrayal. The electoral earthquake that followed was not merely a rejection of the ANC's leadership but a repudiation of what the party had become. It was a moment of reckoning for a movement that had once inspired a nation, forcing it to confront the consequences of its choices and the legacy of its leadership.

Part 2: The 2024 Election

4 Factors Leading to the ANC's Collapse

The 2024 elections will be remembered as a watershed moment in South Africa's democratic history—a turning point when the once-mighty African National Congress (ANC) faced an unprecedented collapse. For decades, the ANC had enjoyed unassailable dominance, drawing on its liberation credentials and its role in ending apartheid to command the loyalty of millions. But by 2024, the party's grip on power had loosened irreparably. It was no longer the beloved movement of Nelson Mandela and Oliver Tambo, but a fractured and embattled political entity, weighed down by corruption, factionalism, and a growing disconnect from the electorate. The collapse of the ANC was not sudden but the culmination of years of discontent among voters, compounded by the economic decline and rampant youth unemployment that defined the country's socio-political landscape.

Discontent Among Voters

By 2024, the disillusionment of the South African electorate had reached boiling point. For years, ordinary citizens had watched as the promises of liberation and democracy gave way to scandals, mismanagement, and an increasingly aloof political elite. The ANC, once the voice of the oppressed, seemed more interested in internal power struggles than in addressing the daily struggles of the people. This disconnect became glaringly apparent in the growing frequency of service delivery protests, which erupted in townships and rural areas across the country. These protests were not just cries for basic amenities like water, electricity, and housing but also a powerful indictment of a government that had failed to fulfil its promises.

The ANC's diminishing appeal was most evident in the erosion of its traditional support base. For decades, the party had relied on its deep connections to working-class communities, particularly in rural areas and former apartheid-era homelands. But as communities faced deteriorating living conditions, with crumbling infrastructure and underfunded schools and clinics, the ANC's rhetoric of struggle began to ring hollow. For many, the liberation narrative no longer carried the same weight, especially for younger generations who had grown up in a democratic South Africa and were more concerned with economic opportunities and tangible improvements in their lives than with the party's historical achievements.

This discontent was further fuelled by the ANC's repeated failure to hold its leaders accountable. The Guptagate scandal during Jacob Zuma's presidency had already shaken public confidence, exposing the extent to which state institutions had been hollowed out by corruption. Cyril Ramaphosa's promises of renewal and reform initially offered hope, but his presidency was hamstrung by factional resistance within the party. The perception that the ANC was unable—or unwilling—to root out corruption only deepened voter disillusionment. Many South Africans began to see the party not as the solution to their problems but as a central part of the problem itself.

Economic Decline and Youth Unemployment

Perhaps the most significant factor driving the ANC's collapse in 2024 was the dire state of South Africa's economy. Years of sluggish growth, compounded by the lingering effects of the COVID-19 pandemic and global economic instability, had left the country in a precarious position. Key industries such as mining and manufacturing, once the backbone of South Africa's economy, had been in decline for years, resulting in widespread job losses and shrinking opportunities for workers. Meanwhile, government debt continued to climb, leaving little fiscal room to address the country's pressing social challenges.

The impact of this economic decline was felt most acutely by South Africa's youth. By 2024, youth unemployment had reached staggering levels, with over 60% of young people unable to find work. For a generation that had grown up with the promise of a brighter future in a democratic South Africa, the reality was bleak. Many young South Africans felt trapped, unable to access quality education or meaningful employment, and increasingly disconnected from the political system that seemed incapable of addressing their needs. This frustration was palpable, manifesting in a growing apathy toward traditional political parties and a willingness to explore alternative political movements.

The government's attempts to address youth unemployment often fell short, hindered by bureaucracy, corruption, and mismanagement. Initiatives like the Youth Employment Service (YES) programme, while well-intentioned, failed to create sustainable pathways to long-term employment for most participants. Similarly, education reforms aimed at addressing the skills mismatch between graduates and the job market were slow to yield results. For many young people, the dream of higher education became a bitter reality as they joined the ranks of the so-called "educated unemployed," burdened by debt and unable to secure jobs in their fields of study.

The economic decline also deepened existing inequalities, creating a fertile ground for political discontent. While a small elite continued to thrive, enjoying the benefits of political connections and access to resources, the majority of South Africans faced increasing hardship. The cost of living soared, with rising prices for basic goods and services placing additional strain on already stretched household budgets. Informal settlements expanded on the outskirts of cities, as urbanisation outpaced the government's ability to provide affordable housing and infrastructure.

For many voters, the ANC's failure to address these economic challenges was unforgivable. It was not just about the hardships they faced but about the loss of trust in a party that had once promised to deliver a better life for all. The ANC's inability to adapt to the changing needs of the electorate, combined with its internal dysfunction and perceived prioritisation of self-interest, alienated even its most loyal supporters.

Covid-19 Corruption and the Poor Leadership of Cyril Ramaphosa

The Covid-19 pandemic was an unprecedented crisis that tested the leadership of governments around the world, and South Africa was no exception. For President Cyril Ramaphosa, the pandemic presented an opportunity to demonstrate decisive leadership and rebuild public trust in the ANC after years of scandal and mismanagement under Jacob Zuma. When the virus first reached South African shores in early 2020, Ramaphosa was widely praised for his swift response. His government implemented one of the earliest lockdowns, introduced measures to curb the spread of the virus, and promised a comprehensive economic stimulus package to support struggling businesses and households. For a brief moment, it seemed as though

Ramaphosa's presidency might be defined by competence and compassion in the face of a global emergency.

However, as the pandemic wore on, the cracks in Ramaphosa's leadership—and the broader failings of the ANC government—became painfully apparent. Instead of uniting the country and steering it through the crisis, the government's response was marred by corruption, inefficiency, and a lack of transparency. The very traits that had come to symbolise the ANC's decline—self-enrichment, factionalism, and an inability to deliver on promises—were magnified during this critical time, leaving millions of South Africans disillusioned and angry.

The Covid-19 Corruption Scandal

Perhaps the most damning aspect of the government's response to the pandemic was the widespread corruption that accompanied it. In the early days of the crisis, Ramaphosa announced a R500 billion relief package to mitigate the economic impact of the pandemic. The package included funds for healthcare, unemployment relief, and support for small businesses, as well as personal protective equipment (PPE) for frontline workers. It was an ambitious plan, designed to reassure a nation reeling from the twin threats of a deadly virus and economic devastation.

Yet, what should have been a lifeline for millions

quickly became a feeding frenzy for corrupt officials and politically connected individuals. Reports began to emerge of inflated contracts for PPE, food parcels being stolen or distributed along partisan lines, and funds intended for social relief disappearing into the pockets of corrupt officials. In some cases, substandard or counterfeit PPE was delivered to hospitals, putting the lives of healthcare workers at risk. The looting was so egregious that it led to the coining of the term "Covidpreneurs"—a damning indictment of those who profited from the pandemic while ordinary South Africans suffered.

The scandal was not limited to a few rogue individuals; it exposed the rot that had permeated the ANC at all levels of government. In Gauteng, senior officials were implicated in corrupt PPE contracts, while in the Eastern Cape, an R10 million "scooter ambulance" project—a bizarre and inadequate solution for transporting Covid-19 patients—became a symbol of the government's incompetence and greed. These scandals eroded public trust in the ANC, reinforcing the perception that the party was more concerned with enriching itself than with serving the people.

For Ramaphosa, the Covid-19 corruption scandal was a major blow to his presidency. Despite his promises to crack down on corruption and clean up the ANC, he appeared unable—or unwilling—to hold those responsible to account. While some officials were suspended or investigated, many cases dragged on with little resolution, further undermining confidence in his leadership. The scandal also highlighted the limits of Ramaphosa's power within the ANC, where his reformist agenda was often stymied by internal resistance and factional battles.

Poor Leadership and Missed Opportunities

Beyond the corruption scandal, Ramaphosa's handling of the pandemic revealed broader weaknesses in his leadership. While his initial response was praised, the government's inability to implement its policies effectively soon became apparent. The rollout of the Covid-19 vaccine was slow and chaotic, marked by delays in securing doses, logistical challenges, and a lack of clear communication with the public. By the time vaccines became widely available, South Africa had already endured multiple waves of the virus, with devastating consequences for public health and the economy.

Ramaphosa's failure to articulate a clear and consistent strategy also contributed to widespread confusion and frustration. Lockdown regulations were often arbitrary and poorly enforced, leading to accusations of double standards and eroding public compliance. For example, the ban on alcohol sales, while intended to reduce strain on hospitals, was seen by many as an overreach that disproportionately affected small businesses and workers in the informal sector. Meanwhile, the uneven enforcement of lockdown rules fuelled perceptions of inequality, as ordinary citizens were penalised while politically connected individuals flouted the regulations with impunity.

The economic fallout of the pandemic further exposed the government's shortcomings. While the R350 social relief grant provided temporary relief to some of the most vulnerable, it was far from sufficient to address the widespread poverty and unemployment exacerbated by the crisis. Many small businesses, particularly in the informal sector, were left to fend for themselves, with little support from the state. The economic stimulus package, which had been touted as a lifeline, was hampered by delays and inefficiencies, leaving millions of South Africans struggling to survive.

The Legacy of Covid-19 Leadership

For many South Africans, the pandemic crystallised the failures of the ANC government and Ramaphosa's leadership. It was a stark reminder of the gap between the party's promises and its actions, and of the systemic issues that had plagued the ANC for years. The Covid-19 corruption scandal, in particular, became a symbol of the party's moral decay, reinforcing the perception that it was no longer capable of governing in the public interest.

Ramaphosa's inability to take decisive action against corruption and incompetence also raised questions about his leadership style. While he was often described as a cautious and consensus-driven leader, these traits were seen as liabilities during a crisis that demanded bold and decisive action. His failure to assert authority within the ANC and hold his own party accountable left many wondering whether he was the right person to lead South Africa through its most challenging moments.

By the time the 2024 elections arrived, the legacy of the Covid-19 pandemic had become a key factor in the ANC's downfall. The anger and disillusionment that had been simmering for years reached a boiling point, as voters rejected a party that had failed to protect them during their time of greatest need. For Ramaphosa, the pandemic represented a missed opportunity to demonstrate leadership and restore faith in the ANC. Instead, it became a turning point in the party's decline, paving the way for the electoral earthquake that would reshape South Africa's political landscape.

The lessons of the pandemic were clear: leadership matters, not just in times of crisis but in the day-to-day work of governance. For South Africa to move forward, it needed leaders who were not only capable and ethical but also willing to confront difficult truths and make tough decisions. The Covid-19 pandemic was a tragedy, but it was also a wake-up call—a reminder of the urgent need for accountability, competence, and a government that truly served the people.

Persistent Loadshedding Under Cyril Ramaphosa: A Nation in the Dark

Under Cyril Ramaphosa's leadership, South Africa endured an era of persistent loadshedding that came to symbolise the broader failures of governance, mismanagement, and unfulfilled promises. What began as sporadic blackouts during the Zuma administration escalated into a full-blown crisis under Ramaphosa, with rolling power cuts disrupting businesses, crippling industries, and plunging households into darkness for hours each day. The electricity crisis was not just a technical failure; it was a profound indictment of the ANC's inability to maintain and modernise the nation's critical infrastructure. For many South Africans, loadshedding became a tangible reminder of the government's failure to deliver on the promise of a functional and thriving post-apartheid society.

The Escalation of Loadshedding

By the time Ramaphosa assumed office in 2018, loadshedding had already become a familiar part of South African life. The state-owned power utility, Eskom, was mired in financial and operational difficulties, the result of years of corruption, mismanagement, and neglect. While Ramaphosa acknowledged the gravity of the problem and pledged to restore stability to Eskom, the reality under his administration told a different story. Instead of subsiding, loadshedding intensified, with power outages becoming more frequent and prolonged. By 2024, South Africans were experiencing Stage 6 loadshedding—up to 12 hours of power cuts a day—on a regular basis, with little indication that the crisis would abate.

The roots of the problem were multifaceted, but at their core lay the systemic failures of leadership and planning. Eskom's fleet of ageing coal-fired power stations had been pushed beyond their operational limits, with maintenance backlogs compounding the problem. New power plants, such as Medupi and Kusile, which had been touted as solutions to South Africa's energy woes, were plagued by cost overruns, design flaws, and corruption scandals. Despite billions of rands in public investment, these projects failed to deliver the reliable power generation they had promised.

Ramaphosa's attempts to stabilise Eskom were hampered by the entrenched inefficiencies within the utility and the political constraints of the ANC. Efforts to unbundle Eskom into separate entities for generation, transmission, and distribution—a plan intended to improve accountability and efficiency—faced significant resistance from within the party, where factions loyal to vested interests sought to maintain control over the utility's lucrative contracts. As a result, the reform process stalled, leaving Eskom unable to address its financial and operational challenges effectively.

The Socio-Economic Impact of Loadshedding

The consequences of persistent loadshedding under Ramaphosa's administration were devastating for South Africa's economy and society. Small businesses, already struggling with the effects of the Covid-19 pandemic and a sluggish economy, were hit hardest by the power cuts. Many were forced to close their doors permanently, unable to afford backup generators or withstand the disruptions to their operations. Larger industries, particularly in energy-intensive sectors such as mining and manufacturing, reported billions of rands in lost productivity, further exacerbating the country's unemployment crisis.

For ordinary South Africans, loadshedding became a daily struggle that highlighted the inequality entrenched in the country's infrastructure. In affluent areas, residents could afford solar panels, inverters, and other off-grid solutions to mitigate the impact of blackouts. But in townships and rural communities, where resources were scarce, families were left to endure hours without electricity, often relying on candles and paraffin stoves for light and cooking. The power cuts also disrupted access to essential services, with hospitals, schools, and public transport systems unable to function effectively during outages.

Loadshedding also took a psychological toll on the nation. The frustration and anger it generated eroded public trust in the government, feeding into a broader sense of disillusionment with the ANC's ability to govern. It became a symbol of the country's stagnation, a constant reminder of how the dreams of the post-apartheid era had given way to the grim realities of corruption, inefficiency, and neglect. The phrase "we are in the dark" took on a double meaning, reflecting not only the literal blackouts but also the perceived lack of leadership and vision to guide the country forward.

Ramaphosa's Response and the Perception of Failure

While Ramaphosa acknowledged the severity of the loadshedding crisis, his administration's response was widely seen as inadequate. His rhetoric about "turning the tide" at Eskom and "restoring confidence" in the energy sector often rang hollow in the face of escalating outages. The government's failure to communicate a clear and realistic plan for resolving the crisis further undermined public confidence, with many South Africans viewing Ramaphosa's promises as empty platitudes.

Critics also pointed to the lack of accountability within Eskom and the government as a major obstacle to progress. Despite numerous investigations and reports detailing corruption and mismanagement at the utility, few high-profile figures were held to account. This inaction reinforced the perception that Ramaphosa lacked the political will or authority to confront the entrenched interests within the ANC and

Eskom that were impeding reform.

At the same time, Ramaphosa's administration struggled to embrace renewable energy as a viable solution to South Africa's energy crisis. While independent power producers (IPPs) and solar and wind projects were touted as part of the solution, progress in integrating these sources into the national grid was slow and inconsistent. Bureaucratic delays, regulatory hurdles, and resistance from coal-dependent stakeholders all contributed to the glacial pace of the energy transition, leaving South Africa heavily reliant on its ageing and unreliable coal infrastructure.

A Defining Failure

By the time of the 2024 elections, loadshedding had become one of the defining failures of Ramaphosa's presidency and a key factor in the ANC's collapse. For voters, the power cuts were not just an inconvenience but a stark reminder of the government's inability to deliver on its most basic responsibilities. The promise of a "new dawn" that had accompanied Ramaphosa's rise to power had given way to a deep sense of betrayal and despair, as the lights flickered off and hope dimmed.

The persistent loadshedding crisis also exposed the broader structural weaknesses within the ANC and its approach to governance. It highlighted the dangers of short-termism, patronage politics, and a lack of accountability—issues that had plagued the party for years but were thrown into sharp relief by the crisis. For many South Africans, the power cuts symbolised the ANC's broader failures, serving as a metaphor for a party that had lost its way and could no longer provide the leadership the country needed.

A Lesson for the Future

The story of loadshedding under Ramaphosa was not just a cautionary tale about mismanagement and corruption; it was also a wake-up call about the urgent need for leadership and vision in addressing South Africa's challenges. The crisis underscored the importance of political will, accountability, and long-term planning in overcoming systemic failures and rebuilding public trust.

As South Africa moved into a new political era following the 2024 elections, the lessons of the loadshedding crisis remained clear. Solving the country's energy problems would require bold and decisive action—not just technical fixes but a broader commitment to reforming the institutions and systems that had allowed the crisis to persist. For the nation to truly move forward, its leaders would need to restore the lights—both literally and figuratively—by prioritising the needs of the people over the interests of the few and working tirelessly to build a brighter, more sustainable future.

The Earthquake Moment

By the time South Africans went to the polls in 2024, the writing was on the wall. Discontent among voters, economic hardship, and the hopelessness of a generation left behind had created a perfect storm. The ANC, once the unassailable champion of liberation, found itself unable to connect with the electorate or offer credible solutions to the country's challenges. The election results reflected a seismic shift, with the party losing its majority for the first time in democratic history. Opposition parties, including emerging movements that had tapped into the frustrations of young voters, gained significant ground, reshaping South Africa's political landscape.

The collapse of the ANC was not merely an electoral defeat but a profound moment of reckoning for the party and the country. It signalled the end of an era and the beginning of a new, uncertain chapter in South Africa's democracy. For many, the 2024 electoral earthquake was both a wake-up call and an opportunity—a chance to rebuild a political system that better served the needs and aspirations of all South Africans. But for the ANC, it was a humbling reminder that no legacy, no matter how illustrious, can withstand the weight of unfulfilled promises and a disillusioned nation.

5 The Role of Opposition Parties

The 2024 electoral earthquake did more than disrupt the African National Congress's (ANC) decades-long dominance—it redefined South Africa's political landscape, presenting opposition parties with opportunities to reshape governance while exposing them to new challenges. The Democratic Alliance (DA) and the Economic Freedom Fighters (EFF), the long-established alternatives to the ANC, emerged as critical players in the post-election order. At the same time, a host of new movements and parties, including the rising MK Party, began to carve out spaces in the political arena, challenging the old guard with fresh perspectives and grassroots appeal. Together, these developments signalled the dawn of a more competitive, yet complex, multiparty democracy in South Africa.

The DA, EFF, and New Movements

For years, the DA had positioned itself as the primary challenger to the ANC, promoting itself as a party of good governance, economic pragmatism, and constitutionalism. Its 2024 election performance demonstrated significant gains in urban centres, where middle-class voters—exhausted by the ANC's corruption and inefficiency—sought stability and competence. In metros like Johannesburg, Cape Town, and Tshwane, the DA's message of clean governance and service delivery resonated strongly. The party's ability to retain control in Western Cape and expand into other provinces was a testament to its disciplined campaign strategy and appeal to disillusioned ANC voters.

However, the DA's journey into the post-2024 political order was not without challenges. While its governance credentials were well established, the party struggled to shed its perception as being out of touch with the majority of South Africans, particularly in rural and township communities. Critics often accused the DA of representing elite and minority interests, a perception the party has continually sought to challenge but not always successfully. The coalition dynamics of 2024 further tested the DA's ability to navigate ideological differences, as it partnered with parties across the political spectrum to form local and provincial governments. While these coalitions offered an opportunity to showcase the DA's leadership, they also risked instability, as compromises on policy could alienate both partners and voters.

The EFF, by contrast, thrived on its ability to connect with disenfranchised communities, particularly the youth. Julius Malema's fiery rhetoric and unapologetically radical policies—emphasising land expropriation without compensation, wealth redistribution, and economic transformation—struck a chord with those who felt left behind in the new South Africa. The party's strong performance in the 2024 elections demonstrated its growing appeal among younger voters, who were drawn to its promise of swift and radical change.

Yet, the EFF faced its own set of challenges. Its confrontational style and controversial policies often made it a polarising force in South African politics, limiting its ability to form stable alliances. While its rhetoric resonated with the economically marginalised, critics argued that its lack of substantive governance experience and focus on populism over pragmatism hindered its ability to effect meaningful change. In the post-2024 environment, the EFF found itself walking a tightrope—balancing its revolutionary rhetoric with the realities of coalition politics, where compromise and negotiation were essential.

Amid the reshuffling of established parties, new political movements and smaller parties emerged, capitalising on the electorate's growing appetite for alternatives. These movements were often deeply rooted in local communities, offering a more personal and issue-focused approach to governance. Their rise highlighted the increasing fragmentation of South Africa's political landscape, as voters sought representation that aligned more closely with their specific needs and concerns. While these new players lacked the resources and infrastructure of larger parties, their grassroots appeal made them formidable competitors, particularly in areas where larger parties had failed to deliver.

The Rise of the MK Party

The 2024 electoral earthquake was not only a reckoning for the ANC but also a moment of realignment in South Africa's political landscape. As the once-dominant ruling party faltered, opposition parties found themselves thrust into positions of influence and responsibility. Among these, the rise of the MK Party was particularly significant, not just because of its dramatic impact on the elections but because of its roots in the ANC itself. The MK Party, named after the ANC's armed wing during the liberation struggle, Umkhonto we Sizwe, emerged as a disruptive force that capitalised on disillusionment within the ANC's ranks and broader voter frustrations. Under the leadership of former president Jacob Zuma, the MK Party's rise was both a symptom of the ANC's internal collapse and a catalyst for its ultimate downfall.

The origins of the MK Party can be traced back to the growing factionalism and discontent within the ANC during the later years of Jacob Zuma's presidency. Zuma, a polarising figure in South African politics, had been forced to resign in 2018 amid mounting corruption scandals and public outrage over state capture. However, his departure did little to quell the divisions within the ANC. Instead, it deepened the rift between his loyalists, who viewed his removal as a betrayal by the party's reformist faction, and those who sought to distance the ANC from his tainted legacy.

Zuma, ever the political tactician, seized on this discontent to position himself as the leader of a new movement. Drawing on his populist appeal and the enduring loyalty of his supporters within the ANC and broader society, he began to lay the groundwork for what would become the MK Party. The movement initially framed itself as a continuation of the ANC's original revolutionary ideals, accusing the party's leadership of abandoning the values of the liberation struggle in favour of personal enrichment and neoliberal compromises. This narrative resonated with many within the ANC's traditional support base, particularly in rural areas and former liberation strongholds, where Zuma's charisma and rhetoric of resistance continued to hold sway.

The MK Party officially launched on 16 December 2023 in Soweto, positioning itself as the true heir to the ANC's legacy. Its messaging was steeped in the symbolism of the liberation struggle, invoking the memory of Umkhonto we Sizwe and the sacrifices of those who had fought against apartheid. At the same time, it adopted a populist agenda that promised radical economic transformation, land expropriation without compensation, and the restoration of dignity to the poor and marginalised. Zuma's leadership, though controversial, proved instrumental in galvanising support. His ability to connect with grassroots communities, coupled with his defiance of the legal challenges that continued to haunt him, solidified his image as a champion of the people.

How the MK Party Destroyed the ANC

The rise of the MK Party was both a cause and a consequence of the ANC's fragmentation. Internally, the party's formation exacerbated existing divisions, as Zuma's loyalists defected in significant numbers, taking with them not only voters but also organisational structures and resources. Provincial and local branches that had once been bastions of ANC support were hollowed out, as MK Party operatives established parallel networks that undermined the ANC's ability to mobilise effectively. In provinces like KwaZulu-Natal, where Zuma's influence was particularly strong, the ANC's traditional dominance was eroded, leaving it vulnerable in the lead-up to the 2024 elections.

The MK Party's campaign strategy further exposed the ANC's vulnerabilities. Zuma and his allies masterfully exploited the ANC's failures in governance, particularly in addressing unemployment, inequality, and corruption. They positioned the MK Party as a movement of renewal, accusing the ANC leadership of betraying the people's trust and prioritising their own interests over the needs of ordinary South Africans. This narrative, though simplistic, resonated with voters who felt abandoned by the ANC and disillusioned by its inability to deliver on its promises.

Crucially, the MK Party also tapped into the growing sentiment that the ANC had become disconnected from its grassroots base. While the ANC's leadership focused on national politics and internal power struggles, the MK Party embedded itself in communities, building relationships and addressing local concerns. This grassroots approach not only galvanised support but also highlighted the ANC's lack of responsiveness and accountability. In many areas, the MK Party's candidates were seen as more accessible and attuned to the needs of their constituents, further eroding the ANC's appeal.

The impact of the MK Party on the 2024 elections was devastating for the ANC. By splitting the vote in key constituencies, particularly in rural and peri-urban areas, the MK Party ensured that the ANC could no longer rely on its traditional support base to secure a majority. In some provinces, the MK Party outperformed the ANC entirely, forcing the ruling party into coalition negotiations for the first time in its history. While the MK Party itself did not win a national majority, its ability to disrupt the ANC's dominance reshaped South Africa's political landscape, paving the way for a more fragmented and competitive multiparty system.

Opportunities and Challenges Ahead

The post-2024 era of coalition politics and multiparty democracy offered both opportunities and challenges for South Africa's opposition parties. For the DA, EFF, and new movements like the MK Party, the collapse of the ANC's dominance represented a chance to redefine governance and rebuild trust with the electorate. It was an opportunity to demonstrate that South Africa's political future could be shaped by diversity and collaboration rather than single-party rule.

However, the challenges were equally significant. Coalition governments, while offering inclusivity, also brought the risk of instability and policy paralysis. Opposition parties, many of which had built their identities in contrast to the ANC, now faced the daunting task of transitioning from critics to leaders. The electorate, disillusioned by years of unfulfilled promises, was more sceptical and demanding than ever, holding parties to higher standards of accountability and delivery.

As South Africa entered this new political era, one thing was clear: the success of the opposition parties and the future of the country depended on their ability to rise above factionalism and short-term gains, focusing instead on building a more inclusive, responsive, and effective democracy. For the DA, EFF, MK Party, and others, the road ahead was fraught with challenges, but it also held the promise of shaping a political order that reflected the hopes and aspirations of a diverse and dynamic nation. The question remained whether they could seize this moment or whether the country would continue to grapple with the legacies of its turbulent past.

The MK Party's rise, while dramatic, also presented significant challenges. Its heavy reliance on Zuma's leadership and populist rhetoric raised questions about its long-term viability and ideological coherence. Critics accused the party of being more focused on settling scores with the ANC than on articulating a clear and sustainable vision for South Africa's future. Additionally, the MK Party's association with Zuma's controversial legacy—particularly the allegations of corruption and state capture that had defined his presidency—limited its appeal among middle-class and urban voters, who viewed it as a continuation of the very issues that had plagued the ANC.

Nonetheless, the MK Party's emergence also offered opportunities for South Africa's democracy. By breaking the ANC's stranglehold on power, it contributed to a more pluralistic political environment in which voters had greater choice and parties were forced to compete on the basis of performance and accountability. The MK Party's focus on grassroots engagement and its critique of neoliberal economic policies resonated with many South Africans who felt excluded from the benefits of the post-apartheid economy. If the party could translate its populist energy into effective governance and policy innovation, it had the potential to play a significant role in shaping South Africa's future.

The rise of the MK Party marked a turning point in South Africa's political history. It symbolised the end of the ANC's dominance and the beginning of a more contested and dynamic era of opposition politics. While the party's tactics and rhetoric were often polarising, its ability to channel voter frustrations and challenge the status quo reflected the changing nature of South African democracy. For better or worse, the MK Party's role in the 2024 electoral earthquake ensured that the ANC would never again hold the same unassailable position it had enjoyed for decades. The challenge for the MK Party—and for South Africa as a whole—was to ensure that this new political order delivered not just change but meaningful progress for all its people.

6 Civil Society and Citizen Activism

The collapse of the ANC in the 2024 elections did not occur in a vacuum. It was, in many ways, the culmination of years of growing frustration and disillusionment among South Africans, who had come to realise that the promises of liberation would not be fulfilled by politicians alone. As the failures of government became increasingly apparent, civil society and citizen activism emerged as a powerful force in shaping the country's political and social landscape. From the work of NGOs and grassroots movements to the energy of mass protests like #FeesMustFall and the radicalisation of electoral boycotts, ordinary South Africans took it upon themselves to demand accountability, challenge injustices, and push for systemic change. This shift reflected a profound transformation in the relationship between the people and those who governed them—a reawakening of the idea that democracy is not just about voting every five years but about active participation and vigilance in the spaces in between.

The Role of NGOs and Grassroots Movements

Non-governmental organisations (NGOs) and grassroots movements have long been a feature of South Africa's post-apartheid democracy, filling the gaps left by an often-overstretched and ineffective government. These organisations became lifelines for many communities, offering services and advocacy in areas such as housing, education, health, and human rights. Yet, by the 2020s, their role had expanded far beyond service delivery. NGOs and grassroots movements became vital voices of dissent and accountability, stepping into the void left by political parties that had failed to act in the public interest.

Organisations like Equal Education and the Treatment Action Campaign (TAC) stood out as examples of how civil society could effect meaningful change. Equal Education's work in challenging the dire conditions of South African schools—many of which lacked basic infrastructure like toilets and libraries— brought national attention to the inequalities in the education system. The TAC's relentless advocacy for access to antiretroviral treatment during the height of the HIV/AIDS crisis forced the government to confront its own policy failures, saving countless lives in the process.

At the same time, smaller, community-based organisations flourished, driven by the passion and commitment of local activists who understood the needs of their constituencies better than any politician or bureaucrat. These grassroots movements, often working with limited resources, tackled issues ranging from land rights and environmental justice to gender-based violence and service delivery. They became the backbone of South African democracy, demonstrating that meaningful change could be achieved from the ground up.

But the growing influence of NGOs and grassroots movements also highlighted the failures of the state. For many South Africans, it was a bitter irony that organisations outside of government were often more effective at addressing their needs than the officials elected to represent them. This disillusionment with traditional politics laid the groundwork for a broader shift in how citizens engaged with power, paving the way for more confrontational and radical forms of activism.

From #FeesMustFall to Electoral Boycotts

One of the defining moments in South Africa's recent history was the #FeesMustFall movement, a student-led uprising that swept across the country's universities in 2015 and 2016. Sparked by a proposed increase in tuition fees, the movement quickly grew into a broader critique of the inequalities and injustices in South Africa's higher education system. Students demanded not only free education but also the decolonisation of curricula, better living conditions for working-class students, and an end to systemic racism within academic institutions.

#FeesMustFall was more than just a protest—it was a national awakening. It revealed the depth of frustration among young South Africans who felt betrayed by a government that had promised them opportunities but delivered only barriers. The movement's success in forcing the government to freeze fee increases and commit to a phased implementation of free higher education showed the power of collective action. But it also highlighted the growing divide between the ANC and the youth, many of whom saw the ruling party as part of the problem rather than the solution.

The spirit of #FeesMustFall inspired a wave of activism that extended far beyond the university campuses. Workers, community members, and other marginalised groups began to organise around their own struggles, often drawing on the tactics and language of the student protests. Electoral boycotts became a particularly potent form of dissent, as citizens who felt disillusioned with all political parties chose to withhold their votes as a way of expressing their frustration. While voter turnout had been declining steadily in the years leading up to 2024, the election marked a dramatic drop, with many young and working-class South Africans opting to disengage from formal politics altogether.

These boycotts were not merely acts of apathy but deliberate political statements. They reflected a growing belief that the electoral system, as it stood, was incapable of delivering real change. For some activists, the solution lay in creating new political movements that prioritised the needs of ordinary people over the ambitions of career politicians. For others, the focus shifted to building power outside of the formal political system, through community organising, direct action, and alternative models of governance.

The Power of Citizen Activism

The rise of civil society and citizen activism in South Africa was a testament to the resilience and creativity of its people. Faced with the failures of government and the betrayals of political parties, ordinary South Africans found new ways to assert their agency and fight for the society they wanted to see. This shift was not without its challenges—activists often faced intimidation, violence, and burnout—but it also brought hope and a renewed sense of purpose to a nation grappling with its democratic contradictions.

By 2024, the influence of civil society and citizen activism was undeniable. The electoral earthquake that year was not just a rejection of the ANC but a reflection of a broader awakening among South Africans who had come to realise that they could no longer rely on politicians to solve their problems. It was a moment of reckoning, not just for the ruling party but for the entire political establishment, which now had to contend with an electorate that was more engaged, more sceptical, and more determined than ever before.

The challenge moving forward was to harness this energy in ways that could sustain and deepen South Africa's democracy. Civil society and citizen activism offered a powerful counterbalance to the excesses and failures of government, but they could not replace the need for effective, accountable political leadership. The future of the country depended on finding new ways to bridge the gap between the people and those who governed them, ensuring that the voices of the most vulnerable were heard and acted upon.

In the end, the story of South Africa's civil society and citizen activism was one of hope and resilience. It reminded the nation—and the world—that democracy is not a spectator sport but a collective endeavour, built and sustained by the efforts of ordinary people. In the face of corruption, inequality, and betrayal, South Africans stood up and took ownership of their destiny, proving that the true power of democracy lies not in the hands of politicians but in the hearts of its citizens.

Part 3: Post-Election Dynamics

7 Post-2024 Analysis: The Aftermath and Implications

The 2024 elections marked a turning point in South Africa's political landscape. The once-dominant African National Congress (ANC), which had enjoyed decades of unassailable power, was thrust into an unfamiliar position of weakness and introspection. For the first time since the dawn of democracy, the ANC found itself unable to secure a parliamentary majority, a stark reflection of the electorate's growing disillusionment and demand for change. What followed was a period of political uncertainty and realignment, as the country adjusted to coalition governments, the rise of new political players, and the fragmentation of the ANC itself. The aftermath of this political earthquake has far-reaching implications, not only for the ANC but also for South Africa's democracy and its people.

Coalition Governments and New Political Players

The collapse of the ANC's dominance left a political vacuum that was quickly filled by a patchwork of opposition parties, alliances, and newly formed movements. In the absence of a clear majority, coalition governments became the order of the day, ushering in a new era of multiparty democracy. While coalitions offered the promise of inclusivity and compromise, they also brought challenges of instability and policy incoherence. South Africa's political system, long accustomed to the centralised governance of the ANC, now had to adapt to a fragmented landscape where power was dispersed among a range of competing actors.

In the months following the election, coalition talks dominated the national discourse, with both established opposition parties and emerging players vying for influence. The Democratic Alliance (DA), long seen as the ANC's primary challenger, made significant gains, particularly in urban areas where frustration with poor service delivery and corruption was most acute. However, their ability to form stable alliances was tested by ideological differences with smaller parties and independents. Meanwhile, the Economic Freedom Fighters (EFF), known for their radical rhetoric and populist policies, capitalised on the anger of disenfranchised youth, positioning themselves as the voice of the marginalised and dispossessed.

Amid this reshuffling, new political players emerged, capturing the attention of voters who had grown weary of both the ANC and traditional opposition parties. Movements rooted in grassroots activism, community-based organisations, and regional interests began to assert themselves, offering a fresh alternative to the entrenched political elite. These new entrants, though diverse in their priorities and constituencies, shared a common goal: to disrupt the status quo and bring government closer to the people.

While coalition governments promised a more representative and participatory democracy, they also faced significant hurdles. The need to balance competing interests often resulted in fragile agreements that were vulnerable to collapse. Policy paralysis became a recurring challenge, as coalition partners struggled to find common ground on issues ranging from economic reform to land redistribution. For ordinary South Africans, the excitement of political change was tempered by the realisation that coalitions, while offering diversity of representation, did not always deliver decisive governance.

A Fractured ANC: What Remains?

For the ANC, the 2024 elections represented not just an electoral defeat but an existential crisis. The party that had once been synonymous with liberation and unity was now deeply fractured, its identity and future hanging in the balance. The loss of its majority exposed the depth of its internal divisions, as factional battles that had simmered for years erupted into open conflict. The party's inability to adapt to the changing political landscape, coupled with its tarnished reputation from years of corruption and mismanagement, left it struggling to define its role in a multiparty democracy.

The ANC's internal struggles were rooted in the very characteristics that had once been its strengths. As a broad church, the party had long prided itself on accommodating a wide range of ideologies, from socialism and nationalism to liberal reformism. However, this inclusivity, which had been instrumental in its success as a liberation movement, became a source of fragmentation in the context of governance. Factionalism, driven by competing interests and personal ambitions, paralysed the party's ability to present a unified vision or respond effectively to the country's challenges.

In the wake of the 2024 defeat, these divisions deepened. Reformists within the ANC, led by figures who had long called for accountability and transparency, sought to rebuild the party's credibility and reconnect with its grassroots base. However, they faced fierce resistance from entrenched patronage networks, whose influence extended into provincial and local structures. The resulting power struggle created an environment of uncertainty and instability, as the party oscillated between calls for renewal and the inertia of its old ways.

Despite its diminished influence, the ANC retained pockets of support, particularly in rural areas and former liberation strongholds. For many older voters, the party still represented the sacrifices of the struggle against apartheid and the promise of a better future.

However, this loyalty was not enough to sustain the party's dominance, especially among younger generations who had grown up disillusioned by unfulfilled promises and a lack of opportunities. The ANC's failure to address the aspirations of the youth—its largest potential constituency—highlighted its inability to evolve in response to a changing society.

The question of what remains of the ANC is one that looms large over South Africa's political future. For some, the party's decline offers an opportunity for renewal—a chance to return to its roots and rebuild its connection with the people. For others, the fragmentation and loss of trust are signs that the ANC's time as a dominant force in South African politics has come to an end. The party's fate will depend on its ability to confront the challenges of accountability, internal unity, and relevance in a rapidly shifting political landscape.

Implications for South Africa

The 2024 electoral earthquake and its aftermath marked a profound shift in South Africa's democracy. While the ANC's collapse signalled the end of one era, it also opened the door to new possibilities. The emergence of coalition governments and diverse political players offered hope for a more participatory and inclusive democracy, but it also posed risks of instability and fragmentation. For South Africans, the challenge lies in navigating this new terrain, holding leaders accountable, and ensuring that political change translates into meaningful improvements in their lives.

As the dust settled on the 2024 elections, one thing was clear: South Africa's democracy was evolving. The dominance of a single party had given way to a more dynamic and competitive political landscape, reflecting the diversity and complexity of the nation itself. While the road ahead remains uncertain, the collapse of the ANC serves as a reminder that no party, no matter how iconic, can take its place in history for granted. It is a lesson for South Africa—and the world—that democracy thrives not on the legacy of the past but on the promise of the future.

Formation of the Government of National Unity (GNU)

The 2024 elections ushered in a transformative era of coalition politics in South Africa, fundamentally reshaping the country's governance and bringing an end to the African National Congress's (ANC) decades-long dominance. For the first time in the democratic era, the ANC failed to secure a parliamentary majority, leaving the country with a fragmented political landscape that demanded compromise and collaboration. Amidst this unprecedented political shift, the formation of a Government of National Unity (GNU) emerged as a necessary, albeit imperfect, solution to ensure stability and functionality in a fractured state.

The GNU was not the product of lofty ideals or

shared visions but of hard political necessity. The election had splintered the electorate's vote, leaving no single party with the mandate to govern alone. The ANC, while still the largest party, saw its dominance eroded by years of scandals, mismanagement, and public discontent. It was forced to share power with parties it had long treated as competitors. The GNU brought together the ANC, Democratic Alliance (DA), Inkatha Freedom Party (IFP), Patriotic Alliance (PA), United Democratic Movement (UDM), Pan Africanist Congress of Azania (PAC) and several smaller parties, forging an alliance that was more about survival than shared principles.

Negotiations and Political Horse-Trading

The weeks following the election were dominated by intense negotiations and political manoeuvring as parties scrambled to secure their place in the new coalition. For the ANC, the prospect of forming a government without its historic majority was a humbling reality. Its weakened state left it in a defensive position, courting smaller parties to secure the numbers needed for governance. However, the party faced significant challenges in navigating these talks. Years of entrenched factionalism and a tarnished reputation for corruption made it a less desirable partner in the eyes of many potential allies.

The DA, despite its ideological differences with the ANC, saw the GNU as an opportunity to diminish the

ANC's influence while exerting its own on key governance issues. Meanwhile, parties like the IFP, PAC, UDM and PA positioned themselves strategically, using their electoral leverage to extract significant concessions, such as control over key ministerial portfolios. The UDM and other smaller parties, while holding fewer seats, played critical roles in tipping the balance of power, ensuring that their voices would be heard in the coalition framework.

Ultimately, the GNU excluded ideologically polarising forces such as the Economic Freedom Fighters (EFF) and the insurgent MK Party, led by Jacob Zuma. Both parties had made significant electoral gains but failed to secure a place in the coalition due to fundamental disagreements during negotiations. The EFF's demands for radical economic policies, such as land expropriation without compensation and nationalisation, were deemed too disruptive for the coalition. Meanwhile, the MK Party's hard-line stance against the ANC leadership, coupled with its controversial populist agenda, made it an unviable partner. This exclusion further deepened the divisions in South Africa's political landscape but was seen as necessary to maintain stability within the GNU.

Challenges of Governing Through Consensus

The formation of the GNU was hailed as a triumph of South Africa's democratic resilience, but it also brought to light the inherent challenges of coalition governance. The coalition comprised parties with vastly different ideologies, constituencies, and visions for the country. While this diversity was a testament to the inclusivity of the democratic process, it also posed significant obstacles to effective decision-making.

Economic policy quickly emerged as one of the most contentious areas of debate within the GNU. The DA's market-oriented approach often clashed with the ANC's more cautious and interventionist stance, while smaller parties pushed for policies that reflected the specific needs of their regional or community-based constituencies. The challenge of aligning these differing priorities frequently slowed decision-making, leading to accusations of gridlock and inefficiency. Key issues such as land reform, energy policy, and fiscal strategy became battlegrounds for internal disputes, making it difficult for the coalition to present a unified front.

Service delivery, long a point of contention in South African politics, was another area where the GNU faced criticism. In municipalities governed by coalition arrangements, the lack of a clear majority often resulted in instability and infighting. Communities that had hoped for tangible improvements following the election found themselves grappling with the same inefficiencies and delays that had characterised the ANC's previous tenure. For many South Africans, the promise of a new political era began to feel like a continuation of the old, as the GNU struggled to translate its mandate into meaningful progress.

Opportunities for Renewal

Despite its challenges, the GNU also represented a unique opportunity for South Africa to redefine its governance and political culture. The coalition forced parties to engage with one another in new ways, breaking down the entrenched divisions of the past and fostering a more pluralistic approach to decision-making. For the first time, smaller parties and independent voices played a significant role in shaping national policy, ensuring that a broader range of perspectives was represented in government.

The GNU also opened the door for new leadership to emerge. Younger, dynamic figures from across the political spectrum began to assert themselves, challenging the entrenched hierarchies of the ANC and other established parties. These leaders brought fresh energy and ideas to the table, signalling a shift towards a more citizen-focused and accountable government. While their influence was still limited by the complexities of coalition politics, their presence marked a significant departure from the status quo.

A Fragile but Necessary Experiment

The formation of the GNU was a landmark moment in South Africa's democratic evolution. It reflected both the challenges of a fractured political landscape and the resilience of a nation determined to find solutions to its problems. While the coalition was far from perfect, it provided a framework for navigating the transition from one-party dominance to a more competitive and inclusive political system.

As the GNU moved forward, its success depended on the willingness of its members to prioritise the needs of the country over their own political agendas. It was a delicate balancing act, requiring compromise, collaboration, and a shared commitment to the principles of democracy. For South Africans, the GNU represented a glimmer of hope—a chance to rebuild trust in the political system and to lay the foundation for a government that truly served its people.

In the end, the GNU's story was one of both caution and possibility. It highlighted the complexities of coalition politics in a deeply divided society but also underscored the potential for renewal and reinvention in the face of crisis. Whether this experiment in inclusive governance would succeed in building a stronger, more united South Africa remained uncertain, but its formation marked a crucial step in the country's journey towards a more accountable and responsive democracy.

8 Economic and Social Implications

The ANC's fall from grace in the 2024 elections was not just a political story; it was a reflection of the dire economic and social conditions that had come to define the daily lives of millions of South Africans. Unemployment, inequality, and poverty had long plagued the nation, but by 2024, these issues had reached a breaking point. The ANC, which had risen to power on the promise of eradicating these legacies of apartheid, found itself judged not only on its political failings but also on its inability to deliver the economic transformation that South Africa so desperately needed. The aftermath of the electoral earthquake brought these challenges into even sharper focus, as the country grappled with the question of how to address deep-rooted structural issues that went far beyond any one party or government.

A Nation's Decline: The ANC's Legacy

When the ANC came to power in 1994, it inherited a country deeply scarred by decades of apartheid, colonialism, and exploitation. The economy was structured to benefit a small, predominantly white elite, while the majority of the population lived in poverty, excluded from meaningful participation in the economy. The ANC promised to reverse this injustice, vowing to create a more equitable society where everyone could share in the nation's wealth. Yet, thirty years later, South Africa remained one of the most unequal countries in the world, with poverty and unemployment entrenched as defining features of its socio-economic landscape.

The ANC's early years were marked by ambitious plans to address these disparities. The Reconstruction and Development Programme (RDP) aimed to provide housing, water, electricity, and basic services to millions of South Africans who had been denied these essentials under apartheid. Later, the Growth, Employment and Redistribution (GEAR) strategy sought to stabilise the economy and attract investment, laying the groundwork for long-term growth. While these policies achieved some successes, such as the expansion of access to basic services, they ultimately fell short of transforming the structural inequalities that underpinned South Africa's economy.

Over time, the ANC's ability to deliver on its promises was undermined by corruption, mismanagement, and internal division. State-owned enterprises, which were meant to drive development and create jobs, became mired in scandals and inefficiency, with billions of rands lost to looting and maladministration. The education system, a critical tool for breaking the cycle of poverty, remained deeply unequal, with underfunded schools in rural and township areas failing to provide learners with the skills needed to succeed in a modern economy. Meanwhile, the labour market was characterised by a mismatch between the skills of job seekers and the needs of employers, leaving millions of young people trapped in unemployment.

The ANC's failure to address these challenges was compounded by global economic shifts and domestic policy choices that often prioritised short-term political gains over long-term economic stability. By the time of the 2024 elections, unemployment had reached staggering levels, particularly among the youth, where more than 60% were jobless. Inequality persisted, with a small elite enjoying the benefits of economic growth while the majority struggled to make ends meet. Poverty, which had been slightly reduced in the early 2000s, began to rise again as the social safety net weakened and economic opportunities dried up.

For many South Africans, the ANC's legacy became synonymous with broken promises and squandered opportunities. The party that had once inspired hope and unity was now seen as a symbol of stagnation and decline. Its fall in 2024 was not just a rejection of its leadership but an indictment of its inability to fulfil its historic mission of building a more just and inclusive society.

Addressing Structural Challenges

The challenges facing South Africa in the aftermath of the ANC's collapse were not new, but their scale and urgency demanded a fresh approach. Addressing unemployment, inequality, and poverty required more than incremental reforms; it necessitated a fundamental restructuring of the economy and a reimagining of the social contract. This was no small task in a country where the legacies of apartheid remained deeply entrenched in land ownership, spatial planning, and access to resources.

One of the most pressing issues was the need to create jobs, particularly for young people. This required a dual strategy: stimulating economic growth to expand opportunities while investing in skills development to ensure that young South Africans could compete in the labour market. Vocational training, apprenticeships, and public works programmes were identified as key interventions, but their success depended on effective implementation and collaboration between government, business, and labour. Entrepreneurship and small business development also emerged as critical areas of focus, with calls for greater support in the form of funding, mentorship, and access to markets.

Land reform was another area where bold action was needed. The slow pace of land redistribution under the ANC had left many South Africans feeling disillusioned and excluded from the economy. While the debate over expropriation without compensation remained contentious, there was broad agreement on the need for policies that could address historical injustices while promoting sustainable agricultural development and urban expansion. Innovative approaches, such as community-led land trusts and cooperative farming models, were explored as ways to balance equity with productivity.

At the heart of South Africa's structural challenges was the issue of inequality. Tackling this required not only economic reforms but also investments in social infrastructure, such as education, healthcare, and housing. Equalising access to quality education, in particular, was seen as a critical step in breaking the cycle of poverty and giving young people a fair chance at success. Similarly, expanding access to affordable healthcare and addressing the housing backlog were essential for improving the quality of life for millions of South Africans.

The role of the private sector in addressing these challenges could not be ignored. While the state remained a key player in driving development, there was a growing recognition that sustainable change required partnerships between government, business, and civil society. Corporate social responsibility initiatives, public-private partnerships, and inclusive economic policies were increasingly seen as part of the solution, though they required careful regulation to ensure that they served the public good rather than entrenched corporate interests.

Above all, addressing South Africa's structural challenges required a renewed commitment to good governance and accountability. The failures of the ANC had shown the devastating impact of corruption and mismanagement, eroding public trust and undermining development efforts. In the post-2024 era, there was a growing demand for transparency, efficiency, and ethical leadership at all levels of government. This was not just about preventing corruption but about creating a culture of service and responsibility that put the needs of citizens first.

A Path Forward

The economic and social challenges facing South Africa in the wake of the ANC's collapse were daunting, but they were not insurmountable. The electoral earthquake of 2024, while a moment of crisis, also presented an opportunity to chart a new course for the nation—one that prioritised inclusivity, equity, and sustainability. The road ahead would require bold leadership, collective effort, and a willingness to confront difficult truths about the past and present. But if South Africans could draw on the resilience and ingenuity that had carried them through their darkest times, there was hope that the country could emerge stronger and more united.

The story of South Africa's struggle against unemployment, inequality, and poverty is not just a cautionary tale about the failures of governance—it is a reminder of the enduring power of hope and the capacity of ordinary people to demand and create change. The lessons of this period will shape the nation's future, serving as both a warning and an inspiration for generations to come.

Part 4: Future Directions

9 Can the ANC Recover, or Will New Forces Emerge?

The 2024 elections did not simply mark the end of the ANC's unbroken rule; they shattered the myth of its invincibility. For many South Africans, the party that had once symbolised liberation and hope had become a relic of the past, weighed down by corruption, inefficiency, and a disconnect from its grassroots base. In the wake of its historic defeat, questions about the ANC's future loomed large. Could the party rebuild itself, regain the trust of the electorate, and reassert its place as a dominant political force? Or would new political movements, such as the MK Party led by Jacob Zuma, and other emerging players permanently reshape South Africa's political landscape?

Lessons from Other African Democracies

The ANC's fall in 2024 was not an anomaly but part of a broader pattern observed across many African democracies where liberation movements have struggled to maintain their relevance after securing political power. From Zimbabwe's ZANU-PF to Tanzania's CCM, the trajectories of post-liberation parties provide valuable lessons on both the possibilities of renewal and the pitfalls of stagnation.

In Zimbabwe, ZANU-PF's failure to reform and its reliance on strongman politics under Robert Mugabe ultimately led to widespread economic collapse and political unrest. The party's inability to address corruption, land reform, and governance issues alienated the populace, much like the ANC's failures in South Africa. However, unlike ZANU-PF, which retained power through electoral manipulation and authoritarianism, the ANC's defeat reflected the strength of South Africa's democratic institutions. This distinction offered a glimmer of hope—if the ANC could learn from ZANU-PF's mistakes, it might avoid a similar fate.

Conversely, Tanzania's CCM provided an example of a liberation movement that had managed to retain its relevance through strategic reforms and strong leadership. Despite its long tenure in power, the CCM adapted to changing political realities by addressing corruption, promoting economic development, and embracing a more youthful and dynamic leadership. These actions helped the party maintain a connection with the electorate, especially the younger generation. For the ANC, this lesson underscored the importance of internal reform and the need to rejuvenate its leadership if it hoped to recover.

The success or failure of post-liberation movements often hinged on their ability to evolve beyond their historical legacy. While liberation credentials could win initial loyalty, they were insufficient to sustain long-term support in the face of poor governance and changing voter priorities. For the ANC, this meant recognising that its history alone would no longer secure electoral victories. The party needed to confront its shortcomings, address the needs of a disillusioned electorate, and rebuild its reputation from the ground up.

The Role of Leadership in Rebuilding

If the ANC's collapse was a story of systemic failures, it was also a story of leadership—or the lack thereof. Over the years, the party's internal factions, corruption scandals, and inability to implement cohesive policies reflected a broader crisis of leadership. Rebuilding the ANC would require not only structural reforms but also the emergence of visionary and ethical leaders capable of restoring the party's credibility and guiding it into a new era.

One of the most glaring lessons from 2024 was the central role that leadership played in both the ANC's downfall and the rise of its rivals. Jacob Zuma's MK Party, for example, demonstrated how a charismatic and controversial leader could galvanise disillusioned voters and exploit the weaknesses of the ANC. Zuma's populist rhetoric and ability to connect with grassroots communities allowed the MK Party to position itself as the true inheritor of the ANC's liberation legacy, while casting the ANC leadership as elitist and out of touch. This narrative resonated with many former ANC supporters, particularly in rural areas and among the working class, where Zuma's influence remained strong despite his tarnished legacy.

For the ANC to recover, it would need to counter this narrative by producing leaders who could inspire confidence and bridge the growing gap between the party and its traditional support base. This would require a departure from the factionalism and patronage politics that had come to define the ANC in recent years. Instead, the party would need to cultivate a new generation of leaders who prioritised service over self-interest, integrity over expedience, and unity over division.

The task of rebuilding also extended beyond leadership to the broader question of what the ANC stood for in a post-liberation era. The party needed to articulate a clear and compelling vision for South Africa's future—one that addressed pressing issues such as unemployment, inequality, and corruption while reconnecting with the values of the liberation struggle. This vision had to resonate not only with older voters who still held the ANC in high regard but also with younger generations who had grown up disillusioned by its failures.

Will New Forces Emerge?

While the ANC grappled with its future, the rise of new political forces suggested that South Africa's political landscape would never return to its pre-2024 status quo. The MK Party, in particular, had proven that discontent within the ANC's ranks could be harnessed to create a formidable rival. By framing itself as the true custodian of the ANC's legacy, the MK Party attracted support from both Zuma loyalists and ordinary South Africans who felt abandoned by the ANC's leadership. Its populist platform, centred on radical economic transformation and grassroots empowerment, appealed to voters seeking an alternative to the established political order.

However, the MK Party's long-term viability remained uncertain. While it had capitalised on Zuma's charisma and the electorate's frustrations, its reliance on a single, polarising figure raised questions about its ability to sustain momentum. Moreover, its association with Zuma's controversial presidency limited its appeal among middle-class and urban voters, who viewed it as a continuation of the corruption and patronage politics that had plagued the ANC.

Beyond the MK Party, other new movements and smaller parties also began to reshape South Africa's political landscape. These movements, often rooted in specific communities or issue-based platforms, reflected the growing fragmentation of the electorate and the demand for more representative and accountable governance. While these forces lacked the resources and reach of larger parties, their emergence signalled a shift toward a more pluralistic and competitive democracy.

The Road Ahead

The ANC's future, and that of South Africa as a whole, remained uncertain in the wake of the 2024 elections. The party faced an uphill battle to rebuild its credibility and reconnect with an electorate that had grown weary of its failures. At the same time, the rise of new political forces offered both opportunities and challenges, as South Africa navigated the transition from one-party dominance to a more diverse and contested political order.

Whether the ANC could recover depended on its ability to learn from its past, embrace meaningful reform, and cultivate a new generation of ethical and visionary leaders. At the same time, the emergence of the MK Party and other new movements highlighted the importance of adaptability and responsiveness in a rapidly changing political landscape. For South Africans, the challenge was to ensure that this moment of political upheaval translated into meaningful change, addressing the deep-seated issues of inequality, unemployment, and corruption that had plagued the country for decades.

The Role of the DA in Shaping the Future

The Democratic Alliance (DA), as a key player in the post-2024 political landscape and a significant partner in the Government of National Unity (GNU), was uniquely positioned to influence South Africa's path forward. Having long positioned itself as the primary alternative to the ANC, the DA's inclusion in the GNU provided an opportunity to demonstrate its governance capabilities on a national scale. For years, the DA had prided itself on its track record of delivering efficient service in provinces and municipalities under its control, such as the Western Cape. The 2024 elections brought a moment to translate these successes into a broader national strategy.

The DA's role in the GNU demanded a delicate balancing act. On the one hand, it needed to assert itself as a credible and competent governing partner, working to stabilise a fractured political system while pushing for economic reform and improved governance. On the other hand, it had to maintain its identity as a party of accountability and transparency, ensuring that the coalition did not dilute its core principles or alienate its voter base.

One of the DA's most critical responsibilities lay in driving economic recovery. South Africa's post-2024 political environment was defined by an urgent need to address unemployment, poverty, and stagnant growth. The DA's advocacy for market-oriented policies, investment-friendly reforms, and support for small businesses positioned it as a potential leader in revitalising the economy. However, this required working collaboratively with the ANC and other coalition partners, navigating ideological differences to implement pragmatic solutions. Key areas such as energy policy, land reform, and fiscal stability demanded innovative thinking and decisive action, areas where the DA's technocratic approach could prove invaluable.

Beyond economic issues, the DA also needed to champion institutional reform. Years of corruption and mismanagement had eroded public trust in state institutions, from Eskom to local municipalities. The DA's commitment to clean governance and its focus on merit-based appointments could play a pivotal role in restoring the integrity of these institutions. As part of the GNU, the DA had the opportunity to lead initiatives that strengthened accountability mechanisms, improved service delivery, and reduced inefficiencies in government operations.

Navigating Challenges and Opportunities

However, the road ahead was not without challenges for the DA. As a coalition partner in the GNU, the party faced the risk of being perceived as complicit in the shortcomings or failures of the broader government. Managing public expectations, particularly among its traditional voter base, required a careful strategy. The DA also needed to ensure that its involvement in the GNU did not dilute its ability to hold the ANC accountable—a delicate line to walk, given the coalition's dynamics.

At the same time, the DA's participation in the GNU offered an unparalleled opportunity to shape South Africa's future. By demonstrating effective governance and championing reforms that benefited all South Africans, the DA could position itself as a party capable of leading beyond the coalition era. This required not only policy success but also building bridges with communities that had historically been sceptical of the party, particularly in rural areas and townships. A more inclusive and grassroots-driven approach could help the DA expand its reach and cement its role as a central player in South Africa's evolving political landscape.

A New Political Era

Ultimately, the story of the ANC's collapse and the rise of new forces was not just a story of political realignment—it was a reflection of the evolving relationship between the people and those who governed them. It was a reminder that democracy is not static but a living, dynamic process shaped by the choices and actions of ordinary citizens.

For the DA, the 2024 elections and its role in the GNU represented both a challenge and an opportunity. It had the chance to prove that a multiparty democracy could deliver effective governance and meaningful change, but it also carried the responsibility of ensuring that this moment of political upheaval led to a better future for all South Africans. As the country moved forward, the lessons of 2024 would continue to resonate, shaping the nation's political future for generations to come.

Part 5: Conclusion

10 Lessons learned and the way forward

The collapse of the African National Congress (ANC) in the 2024 elections marked the end of an era in South African politics. For three decades, the ANC had been synonymous with governance, liberation, and the promise of a better life for all. Its dominance had shaped every aspect of the country's post-apartheid identity, for better or worse. But by 2024, the cracks that had long been evident within the party—corruption, factionalism, and a growing disconnect from its electorate—finally culminated in its dramatic fall. Among the many forces that contributed to this electoral earthquake, the rise of Jacob Zuma's MK Party stood out as a pivotal factor in dismantling the ANC from within. As South Africa reflected on this monumental shift, it became clear that there were hard lessons to be learned and a challenging path forward to rebuild a nation that could truly work for all its people.

The End of Dominance and the Dawn of Multiparty Democracy

The ANC's collapse marked the end of single-party dominance in South Africa and ushered in an era of multiparty democracy. For years, the ANC's unassailable hold on power had created a sense of inevitability in South African politics—a belief that no other party could challenge its legacy or its reach. However, the rise of the MK Party shattered this illusion, exposing the vulnerabilities within the ANC and demonstrating the power of populist movements to channel discontent into political disruption.

Under Jacob Zuma's leadership, the MK Party capitalised on the ANC's internal divisions, positioning itself as the true custodian of the liberation movement's ideals. Zuma's rhetoric painted the ANC leadership as a detached elite who had betrayed the struggle and abandoned the ordinary South African. The MK Party's success in rallying grassroots support—particularly in rural provinces and among disenfranchised communities—further eroded the ANC's base. By the time of the 2024 elections, the ANC found itself battling not just external opposition but an insurgent movement born from its own ranks, one that leveraged its weaknesses and amplified its failures.

The MK Party's ascent also marked a shift in how South Africans engaged with politics. The electorate no longer placed blind faith in the ANC's legacy or its liberation credentials. Instead, voters demanded tangible results, responsive governance, and accountability. This shift heralded the dawn of a more competitive multiparty democracy, where no single party could take its dominance for granted. While this fragmentation posed challenges in terms of governance and stability, it also offered opportunities for greater representation and innovation in addressing the country's deep-seated challenges.

The end of the ANC's dominance was not just a political event; it was a cultural and emotional shift for millions of South Africans who had grown up seeing the party as an inseparable part of the nation's identity. Its fall forced a collective reckoning with the limits of historical loyalty and the urgent need for new approaches to governance. As the ANC grappled with its diminished influence, the question of its survival hinged on whether it could adapt to this new reality, rebuild its structures, and redefine its purpose in a rapidly evolving political landscape.

Building a South Africa That Works

As South Africa looked ahead, the challenges it faced were immense. The ANC's collapse had revealed the full extent of the country's socio-economic crisis—rising unemployment, widening inequality, and rampant poverty. For decades, the ANC had promised to address these issues but had fallen short, weighed down by corruption, mismanagement, and internal strife. The rise of new political players, including the MK Party, offered a chance to reimagine South Africa's future, but it also raised questions about whether these parties could deliver on their promises or if they would fall into the same traps that had ensnared the ANC. However, the formation of the

Government of National Unity (GNU), spearheaded by the ANC, DA, IFP, PA, UDM, PAC and other smaller parties, provided an opportunity to chart a new course for the country.

The GNU as a Catalyst for Collaboration

The GNU emerged as a practical response to the fragmented political landscape following the 2024 elections. For the first time, South Africa's governance became a collective endeavour, with coalition partners forced to work together to stabilise the country and address its pressing issues. This unity, while fraught with challenges, presented an opportunity to rethink how governance was approached. It marked the end of unilateral decision-making and heralded an era where political collaboration and consensus became essential for progress.

The Democratic Alliance (DA), as a central player in the GNU, assumed a pivotal role in driving accountability and policy innovation. Known for its emphasis on clean governance and fiscal discipline, the DA's involvement brought a new level of rigour to the coalition. The party's track record in managing municipalities and the Western Cape offered valuable insights into effective governance, and its inclusion in the GNU was seen as an opportunity to replicate these successes at a national level.

The DA's Role in Rebuilding

The DA's presence in the GNU symbolised a shift towards evidence-based policymaking and a pragmatic approach to tackling South Africa's challenges. One of its primary focuses was on economic recovery, a critical issue for a nation grappling with stagnant growth and soaring unemployment. The DA championed policies that promoted entrepreneurship, foreign investment, and public-private partnerships, recognising the private sector's potential as a driver of job creation. At the same time, it pushed for reforms to streamline bureaucratic processes, reduce red tape, and create an environment conducive to business growth.

The party also played a key role in addressing the energy crisis, which had crippled South Africa's economy and public morale. The DA advocated for diversifying energy sources, accelerating the transition to renewables, and opening the grid to independent power producers. Its emphasis on decentralised energy solutions aimed to reduce reliance on Eskom, which had become a symbol of state failure under the ANC's watch.

In addition to economic issues, the DA's influence extended to institutional reform and governance. The party called for stricter anti-corruption measures, including the establishment of independent anti-graft bodies and enhanced oversight mechanisms. Its commitment to transparency and merit-based appointments resonated with South Africans who had grown weary of patronage politics and the erosion of public institutions. Through its contributions to the GNU, the DA sought to rebuild trust in government by demonstrating that accountability and ethical leadership could deliver tangible results.

Overcoming Challenges Through Unity

While the GNU's collaborative nature provided opportunities for renewal, it also posed significant challenges. The coalition brought together parties with vastly different ideologies and priorities, requiring constant negotiation and compromise. For the DA, balancing its commitment to clean governance and liberal economic policies with the more interventionist approaches favoured by the ANC and other coalition partners was a delicate task. However, the party's participation in the GNU underscored its belief that unity and collaboration were essential for South Africa's progress.

The DA also faced the challenge of expanding its reach beyond its traditional voter base. Historically perceived as a party catering to middle-class and minority interests, its involvement in the GNU offered an opportunity to build bridges with communities that had been sceptical of its intentions. By championing inclusive policies and engaging with grassroots movements, the DA sought to position itself as a party for all South Africans, capable of addressing the diverse needs of the nation.

The Role of the GNU in Fostering Accountability

The GNU's formation underscored the need for compromise and collective action in South Africa's post-2024 era. In a political landscape where no single party could govern alone, collaboration became both a necessity and an opportunity. The inclusion of the DA and other coalition partners brought fresh perspectives to governance and highlighted the potential for innovation and reform in a multiparty democracy.

At the same time, the GNU served as a platform for fostering accountability. With multiple parties involved in decision-making, the days of unchecked power and unilateral governance were over. Coalition dynamics created a system of checks and balances, ensuring that no single party could dominate the agenda without scrutiny. This structure, while challenging to navigate, laid the groundwork for a more transparent and responsive government.

A Vision for the Future

Building a South Africa that works required a fundamental shift in how politics was conducted and how governance was approached. The GNU's success depended on the willingness of its members to prioritise the nation's interests over partisan agendas. By fostering collaboration, embracing innovation, and committing to accountability, the coalition had the potential to address the structural challenges that had long hindered South Africa's progress.

Land reform, unemployment, education, and healthcare remained key priorities. The DA's emphasis on policy-driven solutions, combined with the ANC's deep roots in communities and the contributions of smaller parties, created an environment where progress was possible. However, this required sustained effort, bold leadership, and a shared vision for the future.

The 2024 elections marked a turning point in South Africa's democracy, signalling the end of single-party dominance and the beginning of a new era of collaboration and competition. The GNU, despite its imperfections, offered a path forward—a chance to rebuild trust, restore hope, and lay the foundation for a South Africa that truly worked for all its people. For the DA and its coalition partners, the road ahead was challenging, but it was also filled with opportunity— an opportunity to reshape the nation's future and leave a legacy of unity and progress.

The Way Forward

The ANC's collapse in 2024 was a moment of reckoning for South Africa—a painful but necessary step in the country's democratic evolution. It forced the nation to confront the failures of the past while opening the door to new possibilities for the future.

Whether this moment marked the beginning of a brighter era or a descent into further instability depended on the choices made in its aftermath.

The ANC: A Path to Redemption

For the ANC, the path to recovery lay in rediscovering its purpose and reconnecting with the people it claimed to represent. Decades of unfulfilled promises, corruption scandals, and internal factionalism had eroded its credibility. If the party hoped to remain relevant, it needed to undergo deep introspection, implement meaningful reforms, and embrace a new generation of leaders committed to transparency and ethical governance. The ANC's survival depended on its ability to evolve from a liberation movement into a modern, accountable political force capable of addressing South Africa's pressing socio-economic challenges.

However, this process would not be easy. The party faced stiff competition from emerging and established political forces, including the Democratic Alliance (DA), Economic Freedom Fighters (EFF), and the MK Party. Each of these players had capitalised on the ANC's decline, offering alternative visions for the nation's future. For the ANC, the task was not only to regain the trust of its traditional base but also to demonstrate its relevance in a more competitive political landscape.

The Democratic Alliance: A Stabilising Force

The DA emerged from the 2024 elections as a cornerstone of South Africa's evolving democracy. Its inclusion in the Government of National Unity (GNU) marked a significant shift in its role, moving from opposition to active participation in governance. The DA's reputation for clean governance and effective service delivery, particularly in the Western Cape, positioned it as a stabilising force within the coalition. Its emphasis on fiscal responsibility, transparency, and pragmatic policymaking offered a counterbalance to the ANC's history of inefficiency.

Within the GNU, the DA played a critical role in shaping economic and institutional reforms. It championed policies that prioritised job creation, the growth of small businesses, and the stabilisation of South Africa's energy grid through renewable energy investments and the inclusion of independent power producers. The DA's focus on accountability and merit-based appointments also helped to restore public confidence in government institutions, which had been eroded by years of mismanagement under the ANC.

The DA's challenge, however, lay in balancing its commitment to its principles with the need for compromise within the GNU. While its participation in the coalition allowed it to influence governance, it also required the DA to work alongside political rivals with differing ideologies. This delicate balancing act was a test of the party's adaptability and its ability to broaden its appeal beyond its traditional voter base, particularly in rural and township communities.

The EFF: A Vocal Opposition

The EFF, despite its exclusion from the GNU, remained a formidable force in South African politics. The party's radical platform, centred on land expropriation without compensation, the nationalisation of key industries, and economic justice, continued to resonate with many young and disenfranchised South Africans. As an opposition party, the EFF thrived on its ability to mobilise mass support and hold the GNU accountable for its decisions.

For the EFF, the 2024 electoral earthquake presented an opportunity to position itself as the primary alternative to the GNU. By highlighting the coalition's perceived compromises and shortcomings, the EFF sought to solidify its reputation as the voice of the marginalised. However, the party also faced significant challenges. To remain credible, it needed to demonstrate that its policies were not only bold but also implementable. Balancing its confrontational approach with a clear, actionable vision for governance was essential for the EFF to expand its influence and sustain its momentum.

The MK Party: A Populist Challenger

The MK Party, led by Jacob Zuma, emerged as a disruptive force in the 2024 elections, drawing significant support from disillusioned ANC loyalists. Its rhetoric, steeped in the imagery of the liberation struggle, resonated with rural voters and those who felt abandoned by the ANC's leadership. However, its exclusion from the GNU highlighted the limitations of its approach. The MK Party's reliance on populist tactics and its association with Zuma's controversial legacy made it a polarising figure in South African politics.

The MK Party's challenge lay in transitioning from a protest movement to a credible governing force. To remain relevant, it needed to articulate a clear and sustainable policy agenda that addressed the country's economic and social inequalities. Without this, the party risked being perceived as a vehicle for grievance rather than a serious contender for leadership.

A Collective Responsibility

Above all, the way forward depended on the collective efforts of all South Africans. The 2024 electoral earthquake was a reminder that democracy is not just about parties and leaders but about the power of the people to shape their own destiny. By holding leaders accountable, demanding better, and working together, South Africans had the potential to overcome the challenges of the present and build a future that honoured the sacrifices of the past while creating opportunities for generations to come.

The GNU, despite its imperfections, offered a framework for addressing South Africa's most urgent challenges. The inclusion of the DA and smaller parties brought fresh perspectives to governance, while the ANC's diminished influence signalled a shift towards a more pluralistic political system. At the same time, the exclusion of the EFF and MK Party ensured a robust opposition that could challenge the GNU and keep it accountable.

A New Chapter for South Africa

As South Africa entered this new chapter, the lessons of the ANC's rise and fall remained a powerful reminder of the fragility of power and the importance of vigilance in protecting democracy. The task of building a South Africa that works was daunting, but it was also a profound opportunity—to redefine what governance could be, to address the injustices of the past, and to create a society that truly reflected the hopes and aspirations of all its people.

The ANC's collapse marked the end of an era, but it also heralded the dawn of a more competitive and inclusive democracy. The DA, EFF, and MK Party each played crucial roles in shaping this new political order, offering South Africans a range of choices and voices. The challenge moving forward was to ensure that this diversity translated into effective governance, meaningful reform, and a brighter future for all. Whether South Africa seized this opportunity or succumbed to division and instability depended on the collective will of its leaders and its people. The stakes had never been higher, but neither had the potential for transformation.

ABOUT THE AUTHOR

Michael Mokobane is a seasoned Town and Regional Planner and Heritage Practitioner with over seven years of experience in Property and Project Management. Born and raised in South Africa, he holds a Bachelor of Town and Regional Planning from the University of Pretoria and a Master of Philosophy in Heritage Conservation from the University of Cape Town.

This book is a culmination of his lifelong interest in the intersection between history, politics, and the lived realities of South Africans. It is a testament to his belief in the power of informed discourse and reflection as a pathway to progress.

When he's not analysing political events or championing heritage conservation, Michael shares insightful commentary on his YouTube channel, *Point of Order*, where he engages with South Africans on public matters, policy, and national conversations. His work is driven by an unwavering commitment to contribute meaningfully to the story of a country that is, at once, complex, beautiful, and brimming with potential.

Find out more at
https://www.amazon.com/stores/Michael-Mokobane/author/B0DCJF4TQ2

OTHER BOOKS BY (AUTHOR)

1. The Beauty of Africa: A Traveller's Guide to the Continent's Most Breath-taking Places
2. Experience the Vibe: A Guide to South Africa's Top Entertainment Spots
3. Degrees of Despair: The Struggle of South Africa's Educated Unemployed Youth
4. Where are Men?: An outcry of Gender-Based Violence against Women and Children in South Africa
5. Fun for All: A Guide to Family-Friendly Entertainment in South Africa
6. Spatial Justice: Transforming South Africa's Divided Cities
7. Dream Cities: Reimagining South Africa's Urban Future
8. The End of Work: Automation's Threat to Human Identity

Find out more at
https://www.amazon.com/stores/Michael-Mokobane/author/B0DCJF4TQ2

CAN I ASK A FAVOUR?

If you enjoyed this book or found it helpful, I'd be truly grateful if you could take a moment to leave a short review on Amazon. Your feedback means a lot to me, and I personally read every review to better understand what readers like you need and want, helping me create even more meaningful content.

If you'd like to leave a review then please visit the link below:

https://www.amazon.com/stores/Michael-Mokobane/author/B0DCJF4TQ2

Thanks for your support!

www.ingramcontent.com/pod-product-compliance
Lightning Source LLC
Chambersburg PA
CBHW071038250726

48653CB00005B/1890